Joke Ma

The Ultimate
for 10-Year-Olds is
packed with hilarious,
parent-approved jokes,
side-splitting puns,
and the best
knock-knock jokes ever!

Dedicated to my 10 year old
daughter Ciara Beswick Xx

How do pilots like their sandwiches?

Plane

What do you call a deer with no eyes?

No eye deer!

What did the zero say to the eight?

Nice belt!

Why are ghosts bad liars?

Because you can see right through them!

What do you call a bear with no teeth?

A gummy bear!

Why are fish so clever?

Because they're always in schools!

Why do hummingbirds hum?

Because they don't know the words!

Why was the baby in Egypt?

It was looking for it's mummy

Why don't eggs tell each other jokes?

They'd crack each other up!

Knock, knock.
Who's there?
Ice cream.
Ice cream who?
Ice cream every time I hear a funny joke!

Why don't crabs give to charity?

Because they're shellfish!

Why do scissors always win a race?

Because they take a shortcut!

Can February March?

No, but April May

What do you call a
happy slice of bread?

A jolly roll!

What has lots of leaves
but never actually grew?

A book!

Knock, knock.
Who's there?
Donut.
Donut who?
Donut forget to laugh!

How do we know that
the ocean is friendly?

It waves!

Why did the invisible man
turn down the job offer?

Because he couldn't see
himself doing it!

What's the hardest thing about learning to skate?

The ground

Knock, knock.
Who's there?
Mustard.
Mustard who?
Mustard up the courage to tell you another joke!

What did the big flower
say to the little flower?

Hi, bud!

What do you call
a dog magician?

A labracadabrador!

Why was the teacher
wearing sunglasses?

Because her students
were so bright!

Why did the math book
look confused?

Because it didn't have
the right angles!

What did one wall say to the other wall?

"Meet you at the corner!"

Doctor, doctor I am afraid of squirrels!

Doctor: You must be nuts

I used to hate facial hair

But it's starting
to grow on me

Knock, knock.
Who's there?
Justin. Justin who?
Justin time for another joke!

What do you call a pig
with three eyes?

Piiig

Knock, knock. Who's there?
Nana.
Nana who?
Nana your business!

I heard a rumour about butter

But I didn't want to spread it

Knock, knock.
Who's there?
Wooden.
Wooden who?
Wooden you like to know?

What do you call an ugly dinosaur?

An eyesaur

Why did the chicken join a band?

Because it had the drumsticks!

Where do boats go
when they're sick?

The doc

Why do basketball
players love donuts?

Because they
dunk them!

What do you call an old snowman?

Water!

Why did the pencil break up with the eraser?

Because it kept rubbing things the wrong way!

What do you call
a sleeping dinosaur?

A dino-snore!

Why did the teacher
write on the window?

Because she wanted
her lesson to be clear!

Why did the fish blush?

Because it saw
the ocean's bottom!

What do you call a cow
that can play the guitar?

A moo-sician!

Where did the music
teacher leave her keys?

In the piano!

Why are penguins
so awkward at parties?

Because they
can't break the ice

Why do gorillas have
big nostrils?

Because they
have big fingers

Why did the pancake
go to the doctor?

Because it was
feeling a little flat!

What goes up when
the rain comes down?

Umbrellas

What do you call
a horse that likes
to stay up late?

A night-mare!

What animal loves
a baseball game?

A Bat

Why did the astronaut
break up with
his girlfriend?

Because she needed
more space!

Do you want to hear
a joke about pizza?

Never mind,
it's too cheesy!

How did the mobile phone
propose to his girlfriend?

He gave her a ring

What gives you the
power to walk through
a wall?

A door!

How can a frog jump
higher than the
Eiffel Tower?

The Eiffel Tower
can't jump!

What is a tornado's
favourite game to play?

Twister!

Why did the turtle
cross the road?

To get to the
Shell station!

If you need help
building an ark

I Noah guy

Why was the chalkboard
always tired?

Because it was always
getting written off!

Why do ghosts
love elevators?

Because they
lift their spirits!

What is black and white
and red all over?

A zebra with a sunburn

What do you call
a stolen piece of cheese?

Nacho cheese!

What did one plate say
to the other plate?

Dinner's on me!

I would tell this joke about roofing

But it's over your heads

Why did the lion spit
out the clown?

He tasted funny

What did the triangle
say to the circle?

You're pointless

My friend got crushed
by a pile of books recently...

He's only got his shelf
to blame!

What do you get when
you cross a fish with an
elephant?

Swimming trunks!

What's brown, hairy
and wears sunglasses?

A coconut on holiday!

What kind of star
is dangerous?

A shooting star!

Why did the grape stop
in the middle of the road?

Because it ran out of juice!

What did the traffic
light say to the car?

Don't look, I'm changing!

Why didn't the sun
go to college?

Because it already
had a million degrees!

How can you tell that
a vampire has a cold?

They start coffin!

Why did the astronaut
bring a suitcase
to space?

Because he wanted
to pack light!

What falls in winter
but never gets hurt?

The snow!

Why did Cinderella get
kicked off the
football team?

She kept running away
from the ball

Why was 6 afraid of 7?

Because 7, 8, 9!

What did the left eye
say to the right eye?

Between us,
something smells!

Why was the math
book sad?

It had a lot of problems

I was wondering why
the baseball was
getting bigger

Then it hit me

Why can't you give
Elsa a balloon?

Because she'll let it go!

Why don't skeletons
fight each other?

Because they don't
have the guts!

How do you make
a tissue dance?

Put a little boogie in it

Why don't science
teachers trust atoms?

Because they make up
everything

Ever tried to eat a clock?

It's time-consuming!

What's the best tool
to use in math class?

Multi-pliers!

Why couldn't the duck
pay for dinner?

His bill was too big.

What do you call a dog
that can tell time?

A watch dog!

What do you call a
snowman on a hot day?

A puddle

How do you know
when the moon has
had enough to eat?

When it's full

What do you call a
bear with no ears?

B!

What does bread
do on holiday?

Loaf around!

What's a snake's
favourite school subject?

Hiss-tory

Which animal makes
the best pet?

A cat, because
it's purr-fect

What sound does a nut
make when it sneezes?

Ca-shew!

Why did the banana join
the gymnastics team?

Because it had
great splits!

What gets wetter the more it dries?

A towel!

Why do robots never get scared?

Because they have nerves of steel!

What do you call a
pig that knows karate?

A pork chop!

Why did the student bring
a ladder to school?

Because she wanted
to go to high school!

Why shouldn't you
trust stairs?

Because they're
always up to something!

What do you think of that
new diner on the moon?

Food was good, but
there really wasn't much
atmosphere

What do you call
a sleeping bull?

A bull-dozer!

Why did the golfer bring
an extra pair of pants?

In case he got
a hole in one!

Why was the pencil
so confident?

Because it had
a good point!

Why did the student eat a
lightbulb?

Because he wanted
to be bright!

What is the most
valuable type of fish?

A gold fish!

Why did the alien go
to the doctor?

He was looking
a little green

What did the Dalmatian
say after lunch?

'That hit the spot!'

Why do fish always know
how much they weigh?

Because they have
their own scales!

Where do fish keep
their money?

In the river bank!

Knock, knock.
Who's there?
Atch.
Atch who?
Bless you!

What do you call a cow
in an earthquake?

A milkshake!

Why don't cars ever
get tired?

Because they
always brake for a rest!

What do you call
a fly with no wings?

A walk!

Knock, knock.
Who's there?
Lettuce
Lettuce who?
Lettuce in,

It's cold outside!

Why does the dinosaur
like the bathroom?

Because it's ex-stink-t

Knock, knock.
Who's there?
Harry.
Harry who?
Harry up and
answer the door!

What do you call
a rabbit with nits?

Bugs Bunny!

Knock, knock.
Who's there?
Boo.
Boo who?
Don't cry,
it's just a joke!

What do you call a
donkey
with three legs?

A wonky

What do you call
a dinosaur fart?

A blast from the past

Why do giraffes have
long necks?

Because their feet smell!

What do you call an
alligator in a vest?

An investi-gator!

What do you get when you cross a sheep and a kangaroo?

A woolly jumper!

What did the buffalo say to his son when he left for school?

Bison!

What's an astronaut's favorite key on the keyboard?

The space bar!

Knock, knock.
Who's there?
Olive.
Olive who?
Olive you
and I miss you!

What kind of music
do balloons hate?

Pop music

What kind of room
doesn't have doors?

A mushroom!

Why did the tomato sit down during the race?

Because it couldn't ketchup!

Why don't seagulls fly over the bay?

Because then they'd be bagels!

What do you get on
every birthday?

A year older!

What do you get when
you cross a snowman
with a vampire

Frostbite!

What do you call
the horse
that lives next door?

Your neigh-bor!

What do cows
order from?

Cattle-logs!

Why did the lamb cross the road?

To get to the baaaaarber shop

Why couldn't the bicycle stand up by itself?

Because it was two-tired

What kind of tree fits
in your hand?

A palm tree

Why did the scarecrow
win an award?

Because he was
outstanding in his field

Why did the spider
bring a laptop
to the web?

To surf the net!

Why is there always a
fence around graveyards?

Because people are
dying to get in!

What's green and moves
up and down?

A pea in an elevator

What do you call a dinosaur
hiding behind a tree?

An
i-dont-think-he-saw-us

What do you call a nun who sleepwalks?

A roamin' Catholic.

What did the snowman say to the other snowman?

Can you smell carrot's?

What do you call a hot
dog on wheels?

Fast food!

What stays in the corner yet
can travel all over the world?

A stamp!

What kind of key
opens a banana?

A monkey!

Why did the tomato
turn red?

Because it saw the salad
dressing!

Why was the belt arrested?

Because it was holding
up a pair of pants!

Why do bees have
sticky hair?

Because they use
honeycombs!

What do you call a lazy
kangaroo?

A pouch potato!

Why did the banana go
to the doctor?

Because it wasn't
peeling well!

How does NASA organise
a party?

They planet!

How do you stop
an astronaut's baby
from crying?

You rocket!

Why was the little
berry sad?

Because her parents
were in a jam

Where do you take the dog
with no tail?

To the retail store!

Why did the donut go
to therapy?

It felt empty inside!

What do you call
a sad strawberry?

A blueberry

Why did the echo get
detention?

For answering
back, back, back!

Do you know how amazing
the invention of
the shovel was?

It was ground breaking

Why can't your nose be
12 inches long?

Because then it
would be a foot!

What is an insect's
favorite sport?

Cricket

Why don't elephants use computers?

Because they're afraid of the mouse!

Why did the boy eat his homework?

Because his teacher said it was a piece of cake!

How do billboards talk?

Sign language!

Knock, knock.
Who's there?
Tank.
Tank who?
You're welcome!

What is a tree's
favorite beverage?

Root beer!

Knock, knock.
Who's there?
Orange.
Orange who?
Orange you glad
I didn't say banana?

Did you hear about the kid who drank eight sodas?

He burped 7-Up.

Knock, knock.
Who's there?
Peas.
Peas who?
Peas open the door!

What do you call a fish
without an eye?

A fsh!

Why did the pig cross
the road

Because it was
the chicken's day off

What is the most popular fish in the ocean?

The starfish

What colour is the wind?

Blew

I had a joke about
construction for today

But I'm still working on it

Why was the
astronaut
so calm?

Because he had no
pressure in space!

What does a cloud wear
under his raincoat?

Thunderwear.

Why do potatoes make
great detectives?

Because they keep t
heir eyes peeled!

Why did the melon
go for a swim?

It wanted to be
a watermelon.

Knock, knock.
Who's there?
Leaf. Leaf who?

Leaf me alone,
I'm busy!

Why did the cell phone
get glasses?

Because she lost
all her contacts

Knock, knock.
Who's there?
Howard.
Howard who?
Howard you
like another joke?

Where do roses
sleep at night?

In their flowerbed

Why didn't the skeleton
want to go to the
Valentine's dance?

His heart wasn't in it

What should you wear
to a tea party?

A t-Shirt

Why is Peter Pan flying
all the time?

He Neverlands!

What do you call
a tiger that drinks
lemonade?

A sour puss

Knock, knock!
Who's there?
Says.
Says who?
Says me!

What do you call
a cold dog?

A chili dog

Why is it so hard for a
leopard to hide?

Because it's
always spotted

What's a frog's favorite game?

Leapfrog

How do you get straight A's?

Use a ruler

Where do cows go
for fun?

The moo-vies

What did one toilet
say to the other?

You look flushed

What did the volcano
say to the other?

I lava you

Why are sports stadiums
always so cold?

They're filled with fans

What are 10 things you can always count on?

Your fingers

Why are squares and triangles always exercising?

They want to stay in shape

How do you make seven an even number?

Remove the S

What type of music do frogs like?

Hip-hop

What do snowmen
call their kids?

Chill-dren

Why do calculators
make the best friends?

You can count on them

What kind of ball doesn't bounce?

A snowball

What do snowmen eat for breakfast?

Snowflakes

Who won the skeleton contest?

No body

What did the picture do to end up in jail?

Nothing.
He was framed!

What goes up
but never comes down?

Your age

Why did the teddy
bear skip dinner?

Because it was
already
stuffed!

Why couldn't the
man open the piano?

The keys were
left inside

Why did the nose
cross the road?

It was tired of
getting
picked on

What did Venus
say to Saturn

Give me a ring

Why did the fish cross
the road?

To get to the other tide

What's a pirate's favorite kind of fish?

Swordfish

What doesn't get any wetter no matter how much it rains?

The ocean

What has six eyes but
cannot see?

Three blind mice

What fruit has to
put on sunscreen at
the beach?

Bananas – because
they peel

Printed in Great Britain
by Amazon